Time Flies When You're in a Coma

the wisdom of the metal gods

Mike Daly

Photography by Mark Weiss

Introduction by Michael Azerrad

Design by Randall Heath

 A PLUME BOOK

Foreword

The teenage psyche is not unlike the Atlantic blue crab. In order to grow, the Atlantic blue crab must shed its shell, and during this crucial period of transition, it is highly vulnerable. And that's kind of what it feels like to be an adolescent—everything about you is changing. Even the smallest slings and arrows feel like mortal wounds. The funny thing is, it only gets slightly better when you become an adult—which is where the sage counsel and keen insight of *Time Flies* come in.

Rock music can both help you forget about your problems *and* help you deal with them, and probably the first band to realize this was the Who. They were the band who so famously sang, "Don't cry, don't raise your eye, it's only teenage wasteland." How many kids have taken solace in those ten words since that song came out in 1971? While it's tempting to dismiss the lyrics in this book as the sociopathic rants of bare-chested reprobates (and OK, that's exactly what they are), it's well worth taking another listen.

If the road of excess leads to the palace of wisdom, then metal musicians must surely be geniuses. These guys might have been princes of darkness, but they were sensitive enough to know that a lot of the people listening to their music were hurting. Peaking in the Reagan-Bush era, some of metal's greatest thinkers were ready, willing, and more than able to lend a helping hand to those who were not ready, willing, and/or able to read any of the self-help books that dominated the bestseller lists.

Then again, maybe the whole metal/hard rock self-help thing springs from claims by Tipper Gore and the PMRC (not a band) back in the mid-1980s that rock music was corrupting America's youth. Maybe metal bands felt they had to prove they were actually positive role models. After all, it's worth noting that the PMRC's infamous "Filthy Fifteen" list included many bands in this book: Judas Priest, Mötley Crüe, AC/DC, Twisted Sister, W.A.S.P., Def Leppard, Mercyful Fate, Venom, and self-improvement gurus Black Sabbath. Ever since, hysterical reactionary types have claimed that heavy metal lyrics cause teen suicides, in full denial of the fact that hysterical reactionary parents are actually a far more prevalent cause of teen suicide. Heavy metal lyrics have surely saved far more lives than they've lost.

It makes sense that aggressive music would attract fans who are a bit more troubled than most. It also makes sense that aggressive music might attract *musicians* who are more troubled than most. Sure enough, by a conservative estimate, approximately 76.3 percent of metal songs state that the singer is depressed, angry and/or insane. No wonder teenagers relate to this stuff. As even the most buttoned up soccer mom can attest, being depressed, angry and/or insane certainly doesn't end with adulthood, which is why the profound wisdom of the metal gods endures to this day.

MICHAEL AZERRAD

Introduction

SUBURBICUS-ERECTUS-METALICUS

On April 21, 1986, obsession turned to addiction. It all started innocently enough with four fourteen-year-old boys, one seventeen-year-old older brother, one baby-blue Ford Pinto, half a pack of Marlboro Reds and five very warm, very stolen cans of beer. That night I would reach the most eagerly anticipated milestone of every teenager's life: the loss of innocence, and the final crossing into adulthood. It was to be my first concert: Ozzy Osbourne and Metallica.

After piling into the Pinto clown-car—style and settling uneasily upon each other's laps, we cast off from our faceless New Jersey suburb in hopes of reaching the Meadowlands Arena, or, as it was known to us in the 1980s: The Metal Lands Arena.

Nursing our warm Budweisers and trying not to drop hot cigarette ash on each other we slowly began chugging-slugging up the traffic-choked New Jersey Turnpike. As we stared out the car windows we realized that we were strangers in a strange land, lost in a bizarre sea of suit-and-tie zombies who were no doubt listening to 1010 WINS news radio or, even more afoul of our metal ethos, "dentist office music." Those bleary-eyed commuters, lost in the days before the emotional life raft of Starbucks graced every cup holder of every sensible car in America, were making their way home to their families, while we were running from ours like a pack of young priests running from a whorehouse.

After enduring dirty looks and trading disgusted glares for miles, hope began to gather.

We soon discovered that we weren't alone in our valiant quest. Sprinkled amongst the middle-management losers were others like ourselves—sexually frustrated young men with long hair, dressed in denim and leather. Or, as we were known in scientific circles: Suburbicus-Erectus-Metalicus—the male suburban metal head.

At first we saw only one car of headbangers every few miles, but within half an hour it grew to one or two cars every mile or so. Then, as if suddenly overtaken by a snarling rouge wave, we were engulfed by a studded sea of "our people." With horns honking and devil signs waving we triumphantly clogged every exit ramp within a two-mile radius of the Meadowlands Arena. As the ticker tape parade of metal crept on, our crusty Pinto was funneled into P-16, the parking lot furthest from the arena, on the far side of the highway.

After reviving our pins-and-needled legs and recycling the warm beer behind a dumpster it quickly dawned on us that the only possible way to actually get to the arena was to cross back over the highway through the dreaded "cattle-walk."

The cattle-walk was a 12' x 12' rectangular tube made of splintered plywood and supermodel-thin aluminum that was haphazardly suspended over the breakneck traffic of Route 128 North. Given its seventh-grade shop class design, I can only assume that there were no safety inspections in the 1980s and that Jacoby and Meyers had not yet found the golden goose of the ambulance chase.

I wasn't surprised at the sour feeling that arose in my stomach upon entering the dim, seemingly airless passageway. It was not unlike the feeling I got when I first saw the Sasquatch-like hairy arms of my middle school lunch ladies

All time and space seemed to disappear. We were immediately sucked into the vacuum and crushed up against one another. We felt like we were trapped in a Tokyo subway car—if Tokyo subway cars circulated pot and cigarette smoke instead of oxygen. We were cheek to cheek with what looked like the entire cast of *Mad Max*. Beneath our feet we could hear and see, through the holes in the plywood, the eighteen-wheelers whizzing by like thunderous mechanical sharks in a feeding frenzy. The whole structure was twisting and swinging from side to side as the overcharged patrons would "lean into it" and long stretches were pitch black due to the Jägermeister-inspired smashing of lightbulbs and tearing down of light fixtures. Then there was the smell. The air reeked of a horrid mix of sweat, urine, smoke, liquor, and warm, steamy vomit.

We were suffocating. We were choking. We were dizzy and disorientated. There was the darkness. There was the cacophony of the highway, the yelling, the banging and the destruction.

It was hot, slippery, sticky and deathly claustrophobic.

And just as we were about to slip off the mental tightrope of sanity, the exit finally appeared in front of us. We dashed for the light poltergeist-style, stepping over the passed out and passing by the stepped on to triumphantly burst out into the warm night air. We were instantly mesmerized by what lay before us.

In that moment I knew what Moses felt when he finally completed his terrible trek across the desert. In front of us lay a pure Sodom and Gomorrah paradise. We stood on the edge of an unspeakably beautiful sea of heavy metal sin. Rows and rows of beat-up cars were blasting Crazy Train or Master of Puppets thousands of underage metal heads proudly downed cheap whiskey and funneled cheaper beer. There was an almost angelic cloud of pot smoke hanging over the parking lot like a halo. And then there were the women.

These were not your high school, won't-look-at-you, won't-talk-to you, too-good-for-you-because-their -ex-beauty-queen-prescription -hoarding-moms-and-their-escort-employing-dads-tell-them -they're-the-prettiest-ones-and -that-it's-just-baby-fat-don't-worry-about-it sort of girls, no these were real women—fully developed, scantily clad, and ready to share with you what God gave them.

As we crossed this parking lot-come-Eden, booze was freely given to us, joints were cheaply bought, and magical glimpses of backseat indiscretions were feverishly etched into our brains. Occasionally a beer bottle would glint and glean as it tumbled through the moonlight only to ever so poetically smash at our feet. With wide eyes and sweaty palmed tickets we arrived at a towering fourteen-foot chain-link fence. As we took our place at the end of the line, a leather-clad defendant in front of me turned around and said, "Welcome to the shooting gallery, dude."

"Shooting gallery?" I responded in my Bobby Brady Silver Platters—era voice.

Then it began. A wave of bottle rockets was fired from the parking lot, exploding just in front of us. We crouched down assuming the "Soviet nuclear first strike under your desk position." Then an M-80 exploded a few feet back. Its thunderous boom sent the whole line surging forward. A few airborne bottles smashed on the fence above us and rained down broken shards of brown and green glass into our hair. We pushed forward and eagerly greeted the "turn your head and cough"—like security frisks at the front of the line.

After they searched our front inside pockets for just a little too long considering it wasn't our third date, we were finally let inside the arena. As we crossed the threshold the first concussive wave of Metallica tore through the air. We became like wild animals seconds before a disaster; our senses heightened, our pulses quickened, our pack feverishly hunted for our seats. We cut through the sea of revelers and climbed flight after flight of stairs to finally get to our section. Our seats were in the last row of the uppermost deck, the single farthest point in the whole arena from the stage, but we didn't care. We were swept up in the madness.

The whole arena was feverously headbanging to Metallica. The music was punishingly loud, and the stage was covered with twenty-foot-tall white crosses. People were screaming and yelling and cutting open their seats and tossing the freed cushions around like Frisbees. It was deliciously pure mayhem. Bottles of booze would mysteriously be passed down the row and sampled by all, as girls were flashing their wonderfully naked breasts. I felt like a robot tossed into a lake, my small hormonally ravaged teenage brain overwhelmed by it all. Booze, boobs, metal, boobs, metal, booze, boobs, booze, boobs, metal, booze, boobs, boobs, boobs until it was finally too much and I was overtaken by a profound sense of inner stillness, a sort of knowingness, nirvana, and enlightenment all in one.

I knew then how Siddhartha felt when he opened his eyes after sitting under the Bodhi tree for so long. My eyes were now open; I had found my place in the world, my calling and my peace. I was saved by metal.

MIKE DALY

The music you love when you're sixteen is the music you love for the rest of your life. For being the soundtrack to my wonderfully misspent youth this book is dedicated to all the bands between its pages.

Meditation is one of humanity's oldest traditions. The use of meditation as a way to achieve spiritual enlightenment has been part of nearly every major religion for eons.

Begin by preparing your meditation area: draw your shades and turn on your black light. Sit comfortably in the resonant silence, making sure your spine is erect and your eyes are closed. Take a deep breath in, hold it for a few seconds, and gently let it out. Now, visualize all of the Metal Gods who have guided you to this place and thank them for accompanying you on your journey by making the sign of the devil with your right hand. Hold in your mind's eye the Metal Meditation of your choosing and begin to hear the words echo internally. Repeat the meditation over and over, and each time you do, be sure to turn your (studded) wristband one stud to the right. Let the Metal meditation permeate every cell of your body and feel the healing effect these sage words have upon your body and soul. Remain in this state for 20–30 minutes.

To close your meditation, once again bring to mind all of the Metal Gods who have guided you and thank them this time by making the sign of the devil with your left hand. Take a deep breath in, hold it for a few seconds and gently let it out. Slowly open your eyes refreshed, renewed

Zen Questions are the pathways to discovering one's true self. They cannot be answered by conventional logic because they are, by definition, dilemmas. Thus an answer's validity depends as much upon the individual pondering the question as the question itself, but, be assured when the student discovers his correct answer, he will know it. Zen Questions should be asked of oneself 6 times a day and pondered for 6 minutes, 6 days a week, or, as we like to call it, the "666 Rule."

To begin, find a quiet spot without distraction and repeat your Metal Zen Question out loud. Let the words seep out of your mouth and then savor the silence that follows. Try to "think" from your heart, not from your head. Let your intuition lead the way. Now begin to notice what "answers" start to surface. You may be surprised, startled, or disgusted by what you encounter. But do not fret—it is but your true self emerging from the darkness.

When you come upon the answer that stirs your soul and resonates with every fiber of your being, then, and only then, should you move on to the next Metal Zen Question with a new sense of self-confidence and awareness.

Daily Affirmations play an essential role in our quest for self-discovery. They inspire and motivate us to lift ourselves above our current situation. Daily Affirmations are the tools that help us adopt new attitudes and behaviors that will enlighten our lives by teaching us how to let go of long-held resentments and conflicts.

To start, slowly begin rocking your head from front to back in the appropriate "headbanging" motion. Begin to repeat your affirmation internally in rhythm with said "headbanging." From your heart, feel the words of the affirmation building up and gaining intensity until they burst forth from your mouth. Then, keep repeating your affirmation at the top of your lungs until your voice becomes hoarse and finally gives out. As your scorched words trail off to a wounded whisper, savor your new sense of freedom and empowerment.

ords of Wisdom are age-old sayings worn smooth by time. They have an immediate ring to them, and that ring is the ring of truth. Words of Wisdom can be used anywhere at any time, silently or out loud. They can be pondered during a long drive or used as evidence of one's innocence when the long arm of the law decides to inconveniently intervene during a night out with Jack Daniels. It is suggested that you always be surrounded by these words whether by air-brushing them onto the back of your B.C. Rich guitar or by tattooing them on your forearm. Words of Wisdom serve as road signs on the highway of Heavy Metal life by providing guidance, reassurance, and clarity.